Animals of the Sea

Animals of the Sea

by MILLICENT E. SELSAM

pictures by JOHN HAMBERGER

SCHOLASTIC INC.
New York Toronto London Auckland Sydney

For Benjamin Alden Boothby

ISBN 0-590-00302-X

Text copyright © 1975 by Millicent E. Selsam. Illustrations copyright © 1975 by John Hamberger. All rights reserved. Published by Scholastic Inc.

12 11 10   5 6 7 8 9/8 0/9

Printed in the U.S.A.   07

Thousands of animals live in the sea.
Some live far out where the water is deep.
Many live in the water near the shore.

Storm waves wash some live animals
onto the beach.
Sometimes just the empty shells wash in.

Here is a starfish.
It has five arms and a spiny skin.
If you turn it over you can see little
tubes that move.
They are called *tube feet*.
They help the starfish move along
the bottom of the sea.
They also help it pull open a clam or a scallop.

This is a moon snail.
Its shell is round like the moon.
The moon snail has a tongue like a file.
It files holes in clam shells.
Then it sucks out the juicy parts inside
the clam.

The moon snail made a hole in this clam shell.

When a clam is alive, it takes sea water
in and out of its shell.
In the sea water are tiny plants and animals
called plankton.
The clam eats the plankton.

There are many kinds of clams.
Some are long and narrow.
Some are wide and thick.
Some are smooth.
Some have ridges.

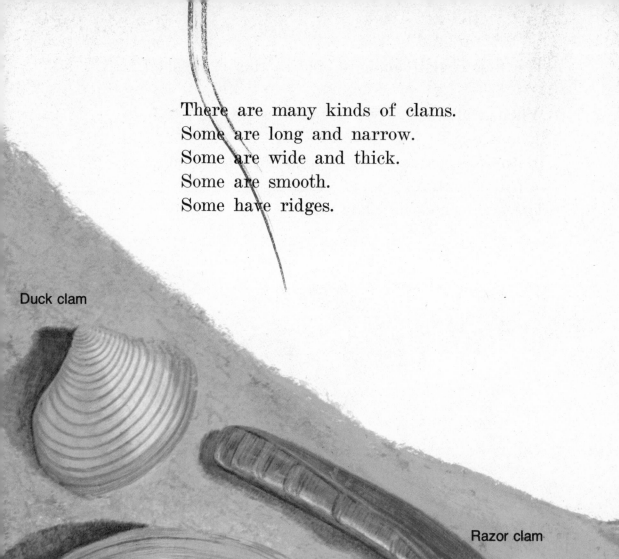

Duck clam

Razor clam

Surf clam

Mussels live on the rocks near the shore.
Their shells are dark blue.
Like clams, they take water into their
shells and feed on the plankton
in the water.

Scallops live in shallow water.
They clap their shells together
as they move from place to place.
When a scallop's shell opens, you can see
something special.

A scallop has two rows of beautiful blue eyes!

Blue crab

Spider crab

Calico crab

Did a crab ever pinch your foot in the water?
Many kinds of crabs live near the shore.
Some have blue feet. These are good to eat.
Some have polka dots on their shells.
Some look like spiders.
These spider crabs plant bits of seaweed
on their backs.
It helps to hide them from their enemies.

The horseshoe crab is protected by a shell
that looks like a helmet with a spine at
the end. It shuffles along the sea bottom
leaving a trail in the sand.

The hermit crab has a way of protecting
itself too. It sticks its soft back end
into a snail shell and carries it around.

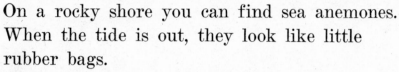

On a rocky shore you can find sea anemones.
When the tide is out, they look like little
rubber bags.
When the water washes in, they open up
like flowers.
But those "petals" can sting.
They sting fish that come too close.
Then the sea anemone swallows the fish.

Jellyfish can sting too.
They have long threadlike tentacles
that hang down below the part shaped
like a bell.
These tentacles sting worms and small fish
and carry them into the jellyfish's mouth.

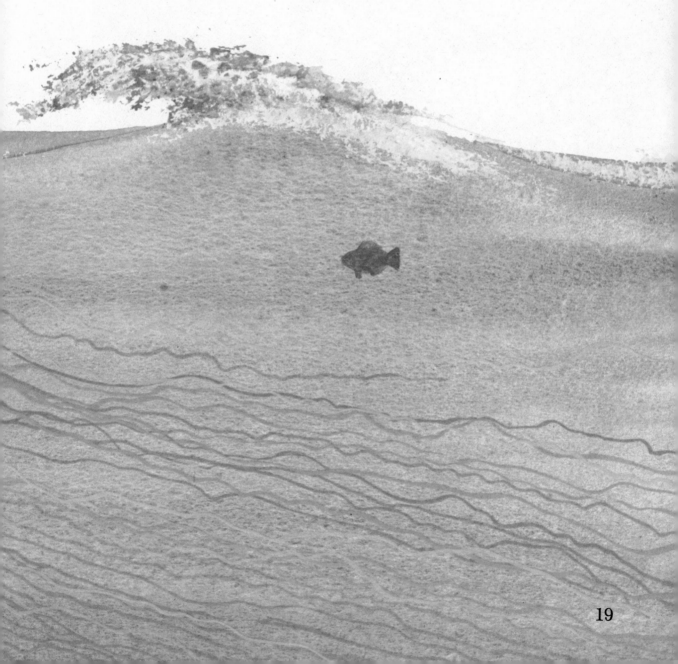

Sometimes the sea tosses up the eggs
of the squid.
The eggs are inside jelly "fingers."
When you hold the jelly up to the light
you can see the eggs inside.

Here is the squid that lays the eggs.
It is called a sea arrow because it
moves so fast.
It usually moves backward by shooting a
jet of water out the front end.
The squid catches small fish, shrimp,
and crabs in its ten long slithery arms.

Squid come in many sizes.
Some are as small as a short pencil.
But some are very large.
The giant deep-sea squid can be longer
than a city bus.

The octopus has arms like the squid but
there are eight of them instead of ten.
It hides in rocks near the shore.
When a crab passes by, it shoots out an arm.
Then it carries the crab to its jaws.
The octopus can wave softly like a
watery ghost.
Or it can shoot through the water using
a jet stream like the squid.

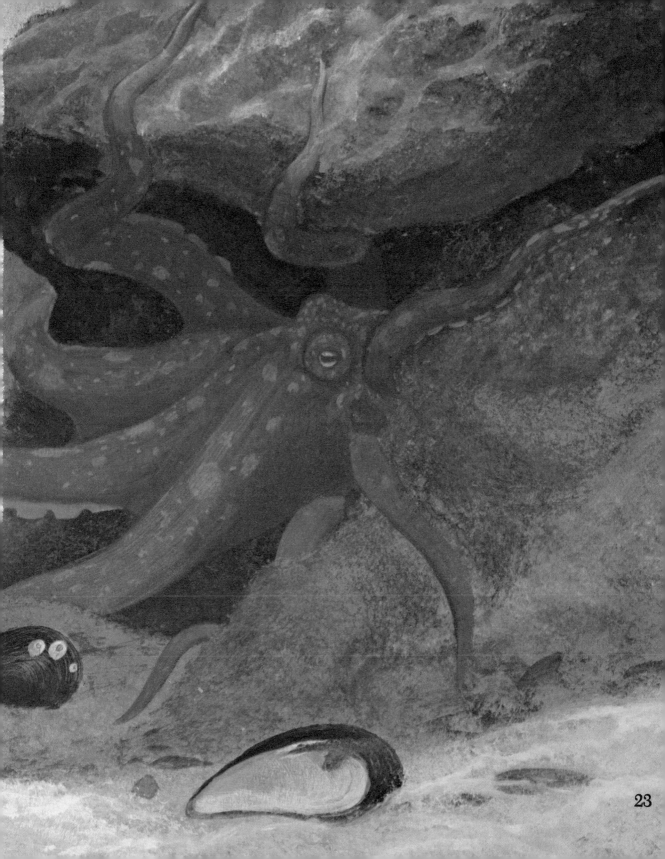

Sometimes a seahorse is washed up on the beach.
It is only a few inches long.
Its face reminds you of a horse.
But it is a fish.
It swims with its head straight up.
Often it rests.
Its tail curls around the seaweed in the
shallow water.

The seahorse is just one of the thousands
of different kinds of fish in the sea.

Further out in deeper water many herring
are swimming together in a "school."
They swim near the top of the water with
their mouths open.
They are swallowing plankton — the thousands
of tiny plants and animals that float around
on top of the water.

Codfish are following the herring.
They swim very fast.
They grab the herring with their sharp teeth.

But bigger fish are following the codfish.
They are tuna.
They catch the codfish in *their* sharp teeth.

A still bigger fish — the great white shark —
can catch and eat the tuna.
The great white shark is shaped like a torpedo.
It can move very fast.
Its mouth is full of teeth as sharp
as needles.

The shark eats the tuna which eats the
codfish which eats the herring which eat
the plankton that floats around
on top of the water.

The biggest fish in the sea does not
eat other fish.
It is a whale shark.
Like the herring, it feeds on the plankton
in the water.

The whale shark is the biggest *fish* in the sea.
But it is not the biggest animal in the sea.
The real giants of the sea are the whales.
Whales are not fish. Most fish lay eggs.
But a whale's baby grows inside its mother.
After it is born, it gets milk from its mother.
Because of this, it is called a *mammal*.
Many whales eat squid and fish.

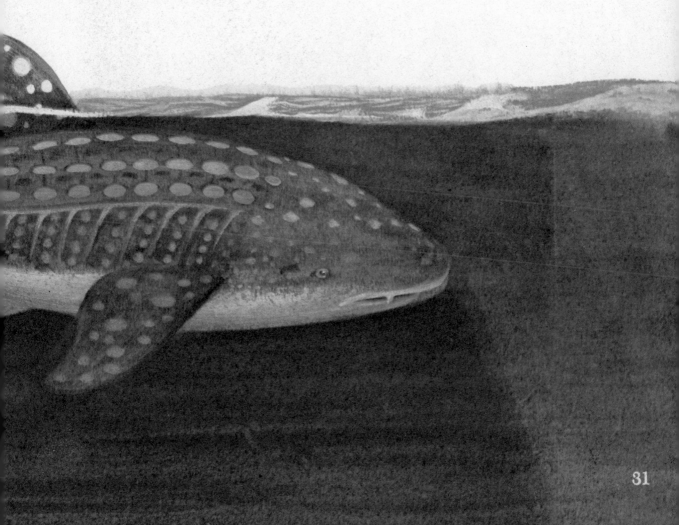

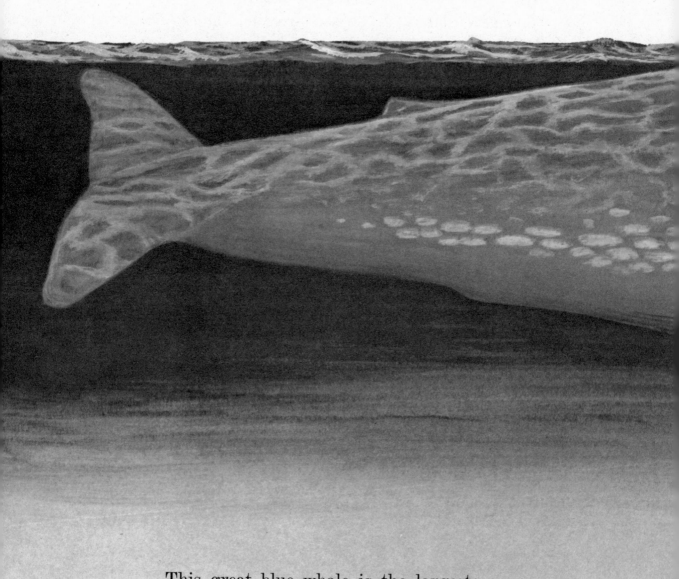

This great blue whale is the largest
animal in the world.
It can weigh as much as 40 elephants.
It can be longer than a railroad car.
It opens its huge mouth — but it does not
eat fish and squid.

It eats only the plankton,
especially krill, a two-inch-long animal
that looks like a shrimp.
It eats lots and lots of them.
A baby blue whale can gain 90 pounds a day!

Deep down in the ocean it is dark as night.
Queer looking fish live there.
Many of them are tiny but have
big jaws and long sharp teeth.
Some have lights on different
parts of their bodies.

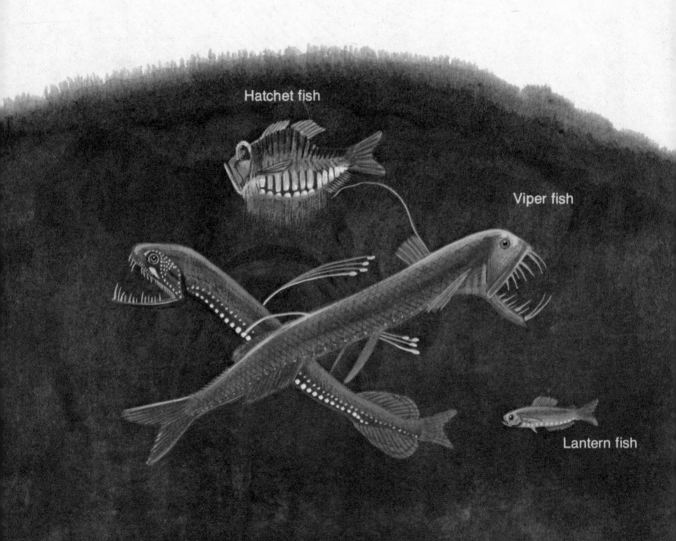

Hatchet fish

Viper fish

Lantern fish

The angler fish has a huge mouth
and big teeth.
It also has a rod that dangles in front
of its mouth.
There is a light at the end of the rod.
Another fish sees the light.
It comes close.
Slowly the light moves down into the
angler's mouth.
So does the fish!

The rat-tail fish gets its name from its long tail.

The gulper has a huge mouth like a pelican.
It has a tail like a whip.
At the end of the tail is a light.
Other fish see the light and come
towards the gulper's big mouth.
Gulp! That is the end of the fish.

The grasshopper fish jumps along the bottom of the sea.
Its stiff fins look like legs.

The black swallower is only a few inches long.
But it has a stomach that can stretch and
stretch.
It can eat a fish much bigger than itself.